Who
says "Twinkle" to the evening stars...

Blessings!
Joan Hutson

© 2012 Joan Hutson

Who says to the morning sun

Who says "Bloom" to flowers here and there, and watches over them with loving care...

Who says "Rain" to the little dark cloud,
and tells the thunder "Not too loud..."

Who says "It's time for rain to go and time to make a big rainbow..."

Who says "Hatch" to the egg in the nest

and starts a little robin on its quest. . .

Who says "Fireflies, turn on your lights,
and give the night surprising sights..."

Who says to the waves on the shore,
"Just this high and no, no more..."

Who says "Scatter" to the milkweed seeds
so in the Spring we'll have beautiful weeds. . .

Who says as the days grow colder,
"Autumn leaves, turn brighter and bolder...."

Who says, "Stars, stars, send down My love

on all who below are looking above..."

Who says to the snowflakes bright,
"Keep falling 'til the world is white. . ."

Who says to the little snowflake,
"I design each one of you I make. . ."

Who says to you and me,

"I love you unconditionally. . ."

Who?

God!

Thank You, God. . . .

Made in the USA
Charleston, SC
12 December 2012